URBAN LEGENDS • DON'T READ ALONE!

MARY CELESTE

This series features unsolved mysteries, urban legends, and other curious stories. Each creepy, shocking, or befuddling book focuses on what people believe and hear. True or not? That's for you to decide!

45th Parallel Press

Published in the United States of America by Cherry Lake Publishing
Ann Arbor, Michigan
www.cherrylakepublishing.com

Reading Adviser: Marla Conn MS, Ed., Literacy specialist, Read-Ability, Inc.
Book Designer: Felicia Macheske

Photo Credits: © Natalie Erhova (summerky)/Shutterstock.com, cover; © courtneyk/iStock.com, 5; © Milkovasa/Shutterstock.com, 7; © iurii/Shutterstock.com, 8; © Slava Gerj/Shutterstock.com, 11; © fenghui/Shutterstock.com, 13; © Willrow Hood/Shutterstock.com, 15; © Richard A McMillin/Shutterstock.com, 16; © slavapolo/Shutterstock.com, 18; © Andrey Burmakin/Shutterstock.com, 21; © Denis Simonov/Shutterstock.com, 22; © SSSCCC/Shutterstock.com, 24; © Kichigin/Shutterstock.com, 27; © Bogachyova Arina/Shutterstock.com, 29;

Graphic Elements Throughout: © iofoto/Shutterstock.com; © COLCU/Shutterstock.com; © spacedrone808/Shutterstock.com; © rf.vector.stock/Shutterstock.com; © donatas1205/Shutterstock.com; © cluckva/Shutterstock.com; © Eky Studio/Shutterstock.com

45th Parallel Press is an imprint of Cherry Lake Publishing.

Library of Congress Cataloging-in-Publication Data has been filed and is available at catalog.loc.gov

Cherry Lake Publishing would like to acknowledge the work of The Partnership for 21st Century Skills. Please visit *www.p21.org* for more information.

Printed in the United States of America
Corporate Graphics

TABLE OF CONTENTS

Chapter One

SEARCHING A GHOST SHIP

Who is David Reed Morehouse? Who is Oliver Deveau? What did they learn about the *Mary Celeste*?

David Reed Morehouse was a ship captain. His ship was called *Dei Gratia*. This means "by the grace of God." He set sail from New York on November 15, 1872.

His ship was about 600 miles (966 kilometers) from Portugal on December 4. He saw another ship. The ship was **yawing**. Yawing means drifting out of control. Some sails were down. Other sails were up. Some sails were torn. Ropes hung loose.

Morehouse watched the ship. He didn't see anyone steering. He didn't see **distress** signals. Distress means being in danger. It was odd.

Morehouse used a spyglass. A spyglass is a small telescope.

CONSIDER THE EVIDENCE

Could pirates have raided the *Mary Celeste*? The *Mary Celeste* was a brigantine. A brigantine is a special ship. It's medium sized. It has two masts. It's fast. It's easy to control. It can sail in shallow waters. This means it can go where heavier ships can't go. It can chase other objects. It can escape danger. Its front is high. This means there's a good view. And it was easier to board other ships from a brigantine. A brigantine is easy to maintain. It doesn't need a lot of men to sail. For all these reasons, pirates liked brigantines

Morehouse sailed to the ship. He circled it. He saw the ship's name. It was *Mary Celeste*. He sent men to investigate. Oliver Deveau was one of them. He was the **first mate**. This means he was second in charge.

Deveau walked on board. He didn't hear anything. He didn't see anything. There were no signs of life. There was no **crew**. Crew means the ship's workers. There were no signs of struggle. There wasn't any blood. There were food and supplies, enough for 6 months. The crew's things were still there. The **cargo** was intact. Cargo means things carried by the ship.

It looked like whoever was on the ship left quickly and in an orderly way.

Deveau said the ship was a "wet mess."

The **cabins** were flooded. Cabins are rooms on a ship. There was about 4 feet (1.2 meters) of water. But the ship still could have sailed.

There was a missing lifeboat. There were two open hatches. A pump was taken apart. There was a missing rope. This rope raised the main sail.

Navigational tools were missing. These tools find places. Most of the ship's papers were missing. Maps were there. But they were tossed around. The ship's **logbook** was there. Logbooks are travel diaries. The last entry was 9 days earlier. It stated that the ship was close to islands near Portugal.

Chapter Two

AN UNLUCKY SHIP

What are the origins of the *Mary Celeste*?
Why is the *Mary Celeste* unlucky?

The *Dei Gratia* had discovered a **ghost ship**. This is a ship found sailing without the crew. The *Mary Celeste* became famous. People wondered what happened. Why would the crew leave a **seaworthy** ship? Seaworthy means in good shape. It was able to sail without sinking.

The *Mary Celeste* was built in Nova Scotia. This is in Canada. The ship was built in 1861. It was first called the *Amazon*. The British owned it. Then, the

United States bought it in 1868. The ship got a new name. It became *Mary Celeste*. It had many owners. One owner said the *Mary Celeste* was "the most unlucky" ship.

The *Mary Celeste* was about 100 feet (30.5 m) long.

SPOTLIGHT

BIOGRAPHY

Dr. James P. Delgado is a maritime historian. This means he studies history of sea events. He's also a marine archaeologist. This means he studies shipwrecks. He's explored many ships. After Gibraltar, many owners bought the *Mary Celeste*. The last owner crashed the ship. Delgado thinks he found it. He said, "The final resting place of the infamous *Mary Celeste* has been found." The ship's remains were damaged. They were covered with coral. They were on a reef in Haiti. Delgado studied the wood. He matched it to the same trees used to build the *Mary Celeste*. Other experts don't think the wood matches.

The *Mary Celeste* was doomed. The first captain was Robert McLellan. He got really sick. This happened days after he took command. He died at the beginning of his first trip. He was the first of three captains to die.

John Nutting Parker was the second captain. He hit a fishing boat. He ran into another ship. That ship sank.

Other bad things happened. One example is when the *Mary Celeste* was driven ashore. This happened in a storm. It was badly damaged. It was **abandoned** as a wreck. Abandon means to leave. Another example happened in a shipyard. It was being fixed. A fire broke out.

Its first voyage was to carry timber across the Atlantic to London.

Chapter Three

ABANDON SHIP!

Who is Benjamin Spooner Briggs? What happened to the *Mary Celeste*? What happened at Gibraltar?

Benjamin Spooner Briggs was a skilled sailor. He was the son of a sea captain. He had a lot of experience. He was brave. He was fair. He was well-liked. He took command of the *Mary Celeste* in 1872. He hired the best crew. He hired seven men. He trusted them. He brought his wife, Sarah. He also brought his daughter, Sophia. Sophia was 2 years old.

Briggs was religious. He did not drink alcohol. So, his first mission was odd. He transported 1,701 barrels of alcohol. The alcohol was really strong. It was too strong to drink.

Briggs left his son in Massachusetts. He stayed with his grandmother.

The *Mary Celeste* crew vanished without a trace.

Briggs and Morehouse were friends. They had sailed together in the past. Before leaving, they had dinner. Then Briggs set sail from Staten Island. This is in New York. It was November 7, 1872. He traveled to Genoa, Italy.

The *Mary Celeste* had a bad start. There was a storm. The ship had to **anchor**. Anchor means to stay in one place. The ship couldn't move for 2 days. It had bad weather for 2 weeks. After that, no one knows what happened.

Briggs was never seen again. Neither was his family. Neither was his crew. They never made it to Italy.

Gibraltar is on the coast of Spain. It has a busy port.

The *Dei Gratia* found the ship. Deveau asked Morehouse to take it to Gibraltar. He wanted the **salvage** rights. Salvage means property saved from destruction. People got paid for finding lost ships. Deveau thought he'd make a lot of money.

Morehouse agreed. He divided his crew. Three men sailed on the *Mary Celeste*. The rest sailed on the *Dei Gratia*. They made slow progress.

Deveau fixed the *Mary Celeste*'s **rigging**. Rigging means ropes and sails. He did this in 3 days. Then, he set sail. The *Dei Gratia* landed on December 12, 1872. The *Mary Celeste* faced fog. It came the next day. It landed on Friday the 13th.

REAL-WORLD CONNECTION

There was a ship. It was named the *Purple Beach*. It was heading to Germany. It was about 20 miles (32 km) off the coast. It had 6,000 tons of fertilizer. Fertilizer is special soil. It's a chemical mixture. It can be dangerous. A fire broke out. Thick smoke rose above the ship. Fumes were released into the air. Fumes were poisonous. The crew got worried. They thought the ship could explode. They abandoned the ship. People in nearby towns got worried. They smelled something bad. They kept windows closed. They kept doors closed. Over 20 people went to the hospital. This happened in 2015.

Chapter Four

UNUSUAL SUSPECTS

What happened at Gibraltar? What are other ideas about the mystery of the *Mary Celeste*?

Deveau didn't become a hero. He became a **suspect**. Suspects are accused of crimes. People thought Deveau and his men killed the *Mary Celeste*'s crew.

There was a trial. A judge determined if the crew should get money. The lawyer thought there was foul play. He couldn't believe that Briggs would abandon his ship. He investigated for 3 months. He didn't find any proof. So, the crew got a little money. But their

reputation was ruined. Reputation means what people think of you. The crew felt bad. They were punished for a crime they didn't do.

Some sources say the lawyer found a sword with blood. It turned out to be rust.

No one knows what happened to Briggs and his crew. There are many ideas. Some think **pirates** attacked. Pirates are sea robbers. They could've killed the crew. But this didn't make sense. Pirates steal things. The ship was intact. All the ship's things were there. And there were no dead bodies.

There were nine empty barrels. Some think there was a **mutiny**. Mutiny means the crew took over the captain's power. The crew got drunk. They killed Briggs. Then, they escaped on a lifeboat. But where was the crew? Where were the dead bodies?

Some think Morehouse and Briggs worked together to split the salvage rights

INVESTIGATION TIPS

- Talk to someone who knows about ships.
- Use tools to study shipwrecks. A magnetometer finds iron or magnetic metals. An ultraviolet light finds blood that can't be seen. A side-scan takes pictures underwater.
- Learn about gas chromatography. This is a scientific process. It finds out what's in gas. Study the air trapped in ships.
- Study world maps. Study locations of bodies of water.
- Talk to insurance companies. Find out what's on wrecked ships.
- Read about shipwrecks. Read logbooks. Read letters. Learn everything you can. Look for clues.
- Learn to swim. Learn to dive. Be safe and comfortable in water.

Some have blamed sea monsters and aliens.

Abel Fosdyk said he was a survivor. He said he worked on the *Mary Celeste*. He said there was a swimming contest. A stage was built to watch. People stood on it. The stage broke. People slid into the sea. Sharks ate them all. Fosdyk said he wasn't on the stage. He left in the lifeboat. (There were many mistakes in his story.)

Some people think a giant octopus attacked. The octopus took one person at a time. It ate everybody. Giant squids have attacked ships. Some say they've eaten people. But why would they take things like navigational tools?

Chapter Five

BLAMING SCIENCE AND NATURE

What's a scientific explanation? What are natural explanations?

Science may explain the mystery. Nine barrels were empty. They were made of red oak. The rest were made of white oak. Red oak is more **porous**. Porous means having tiny holes. Air or water can get through. So, alcohol could've leaked out. It **evaporates**. This means it turns to fumes. Steel bands are on the barrels. They might have hit each other as the ship moved. This would cause sparks. This could lead to an explosion. This may have scared the crew. Briggs could've put them on a lifeboat. He might have wanted them to stay away for a little bit. But the lifeboat drifted away.

Captains wouldn't abandon their ships unless they had to.

EXPLAINED BY SCIENCE

Objects float or sink. Buoyancy is a science concept. It's the force that causes floating. Heavy ships push down into water. They make a downward push. This pushes water aside. It displaces water. The water around ships pushes upward. It pushes against ships. This pushing is a force. It's called upthrust. The size of the upthrust depends on the ship. Bigger ships push more water up. The upthrust becomes the same as the ship's weight. This is how ships float. Heavier ships weigh more. They need to sink more. This makes more upthrust to balance weight.

Nature could be blamed. The ship could've hit a **waterspout**. A waterspout is a tornado at sea. A waterspout floods ships. Briggs might have thought the ship was sinking.

Some people think there was a **seaquake**. A seaquake is an earthquake in the seabed. This would make the ship rock a lot more than normal. This would damage parts of the cargo.

There are different ideas for how the crew got on the lifeboat. They wouldn't survive. They had no supplies. They were in the open seas. But what really happened? It doesn't matter. The *Mary Celeste* lives in people's imaginations.

Waterspouts can pull fish and other animals from the water into the sky.

DID YOU KNOW?

- The *Dei Gratia* set sail 8 days after the *Mary Celeste*. They followed the same path.
- Captain Briggs's wife brought a piano. The piano was dry. It was in good condition.
- In 1885, the last captain of the *Mary Celeste* crashed on purpose. The captain wrecked the ship in Haiti. He wanted to collect insurance money. This was fraud. It's a crime.
- Sir Arthur Conan Doyle was a writer. He's famous for his Sherlock Holmes stories. He wrote a book about the *Mary Celeste*. He called it the *Marie Celeste*. That name stuck. Many people confused the ship's real name. They called it the *Marie Celeste*.
- An anagram is a word game. It's when letters are rearranged. New words are formed. There's a clever anagram of "Mary Celeste." It is: "met scary eel." Some people think this is proof of a sea monster attack.
- Captain Benjamin Spooner Briggs was going to quit sea life. He was going to buy a hardware store. Hardware means tools and items. This was a year before he captained the *Mary Celeste*.
- Clive Cussler is a writer. He created the National Underwater and Marine Agency. This was a fictional organization in his stories. Then, he made it real. He funds it. The agency is a group that finds shipwrecks.
- The most famous ghost ship is the *Flying Dutchman*. It haunts the waters near the Cape of Good Hope. This is in South Africa.

CONSIDER THIS!

Take a Position: **What happened to the *Mary Celeste*? Reread Chapters Four and Five. Which explanation makes the most sense? Argue your point with reasons and evidence.**

Say What? **Read the 45th Parallel Press book about the Roanoke Colony. Compare the *Mary Celeste* to the Roanoke colonists. Explain how they're alike. Explain how they're different.**

Think About It! **Read the 45th Parallel Press book about the Bermuda Triangle. How are the *Mary Celeste* and the Bermuda Triangle connected? Could the *Mary Celeste* have gotten trapped in the Bermuda Triangle?**

LEARN MORE

- Krasner, Barbara. *Mystery of the Mary Celeste*. Minneapolis: ABDO, 2016.
- MacLeod, Elizabeth. *Vanished: True Tales of Mysterious Disappearances*. Toronto: Annick Press, 2016.
- Yolen, Jane, Heidi Stemple, and Roger Roth (illustrator). *The Mary Celeste: An Unsolved Mystery from History*. New York: Simon & Schuster Books for Young Readers, 2002.

GLOSSARY

abandoned (uh-BAN-duhnd) left

anchor (ANG-kur) to stay in one place for a while

cabins (KAB-inz) rooms on a ship

cargo (KAHR-goh) the things carried and transported by a ship

crew (KROO) people who work on a ship

distress (dih-STRES) being in danger

evaporates (ih-VAP-uh-rates) becomes gas

first mate (FURST MATE) second in command of a ship

ghost ship (GOHST SHIP) a ship found sailing without the crew

logbook (LAWG-buk) travel diary that records a ship's progress, repairs, and more

mutiny (MYOO-tuh-nee) the takeover of someone's command

navigational (nav-ih-GAY-shun-uhl) related to the finding or locating of things

pirates (PYE-rits) sea robbers

porous (POR-uhs) having tiny holes that allow air or water to escape

reputation (rep-yuh-TAY-shuhn) opinions held about someone or something

rigging (RIG-ing) a ship's ropes and sails

salvage (SAL-vij) property saved from destruction

seaquake (SEE-kwake) an earthquake on the seabed

seaworthy (SEE-wur-thee) able to sail the seas, a ship in good shape

suspect (SUHS-pekt) a person accused of committing a crime

waterspout (WAW-tur-spout) tornado at sea

yawing (YAW-ing) drifting out of control

INDEX

ABOUT THE AUTHOR

Dr. Virginia Loh-Hagan is an author, university professor, former classroom teacher, and curriculum designer. She doesn't like to get on ships. She gets seasick. She lives in San Diego with her very tall husband and very naughty dogs. To learn more about her, visit www.virginialoh.com.